DATE DUE

Christmas in Russia

Christmas in Russia

Christmas Around the World
From World Book

World Book, Inc.
a Scott Fetzer company

Chicago

Christmas in Russia was created by the Editorial and
Art departments of World Book Publishing.

World Book, Inc.
233 N. Michigan Ave.
Chicago, IL 60601

Every effort has been made to locate copyright holders of
material in this volume.

For information on other World Book products, call
1-800-WORLDBK (967-5325), or visit our Web site at
www.worldbook.com

World Book Publishing and World Book Direct Marketing
wish to thank the following individuals for their contributions
to *Christmas in Russia:* Mariana Beliayeva, Karen Ingebretsen,
Rebecca A. Lauer, and Natalia G. Toreeva. Special thanks also
go to the following staff members of the Great Encyclopedia of
Russia Publishing House: Dr. Aleksandr Gorkin, Felix
Kreynin, Dr. Viktor Panov, Dr. Vladimir Petrukhin, and
Natalia Zaremba.

ISBN: 0-7166-0862-6
LC: 2001086230

Printed in Singapore

6 7 8 9 10 01

Contents

Part I

Christmas in Old Russia

In a passage from his classic novel, *War and Peace* (1869), Leo Tolstoy paints a vivid picture of Christmas in old Russia. His characters, like their real-life counterparts of the 1800's, eagerly looked forward to *Sviatki* (the Christmas season) and celebrated it by going *mumming*.

Mumming was a popular Christmas custom in old Russia among

The Christmas scene in *War and Peace* starts with a group of mummers—serfs, in this case—boldly crashing a gathering at the home of a nobleman. The mummers—dressed as bears, Turks, tavern keepers, and other comic or fearsome characters—dance, frolic, and generally make merry. Their high spirits are catching, and soon the young aristocrats of the house put on their own mummers' garb and join in the fun.

Two troikas dash through the Siberian countryside. Sleighs were the traditional form of transportation during the long winters in old Russia.

young people from every level of society. They enjoyed the tradition of dressing up in colorful costumes and clowning around for the amusement of their neighbors.

Ready to make a night of it, they all trudge out in the snow and climb into their *troikas*. Troikas are lightweight sleighs pulled by three horses. They speed through the snow at a fast clip, their tinkling bells announcing to all that a sleigh is rapidly approaching.

The group of mummers make their way to a neighbor's house, where their costumes cause much merriment, and they vie with each other to see who has the best disguise. Eventually, a space is cleared for the visitors, and refreshments are served. Then the whole group—peasants and aristocrats alike—takes part in Russian country dances and *gadanie* (guessing games). Finally, everyone sits down to a huge feast—the serfs in the ballroom and the nobles in the drawing room.

Tolstoy gives us a picturesque but historically accurate account of Christmas in Russia in the early 1800's, with its snowbanks, frosty air, sleigh bells, and men and women dressed in sable. We can imagine the outrageous costumes of the mummers and the uproarious parties and games, as well as the brief social equality between serf and aristocrat.

In those days, when the *czars* (Russian emperors) ruled Russia, Christmas was as colorful as old Russia itself. It was a happy, festive time when people decorated Christmas trees, feasted, exchanged gifts, and enjoyed the company of friends and family. But above all, Christmas was one of the holiest days of the year, second only to Easter in the Russian Orthodox Church, the official church of the nation.

Christmas in Russia during this period was celebrated on December 25, just as it was throughout the rest of the world, and the much-loved Sviatki season lasted from December 25 through January 7. But that was changed in 1917, when most of the world adopted the Gregorian calendar, and the Russian Orthodox Church, for its own uses, preserved the old Julian calendar. The old Julian calendar was 13 days behind the Gregorian calendar, so after the

> *In those days. . . .Christmas was as colorful as old Russia itself. It was a happy, festive time when people decorated Christmas trees, feasted, exchanged gifts, and enjoyed the company of friends and family.*

1917 revolution, Christmas was officially celebrated on January 7. To this day, Russians celebrate Christmas after New Year's.

Russian Christmas celebrations are steeped in old Slavic customs mixed with Eastern Orthodox traditions. They are at once strange and familiar, a rich and unique blend of centuries-old pagan rituals and European festivals.

The Russian climate cooperates with tradition and provides a "white

Christmas." Deep snow covers Moscow and St. Petersburg in winter, as well as most of the rest of the country. Many of Russia's rivers, lakes, and coastal waters are frozen for months, and the landscape looks like a winter wonderland. The scenery could easily have inspired a Christmas card or two, with its horse-drawn sleighs, graceful ice skaters, and rosy-cheeked children bundled in winter clothes.

To fully understand Christmas customs in old Russia, we need to know something of the history of that era. In the 1800's, Russia was ruled by *czars,* emperors whose power over all Russia was complete. *Serfdom,* in which peasants were legally bound to the land, was the economic basis of Russian power.

Nicholas II, the last czar of Russia, was absolute ruler of more than 120 million people in a kingdom that extended from the Arctic Ocean south to the Black Sea, and from the Baltic Sea east to the Pacific Ocean. It was an area that covered more than 6-1/2 million square miles (17,000 square kilometers) — one-sixth of the earth.

The population of Russia during Nicholas II's reign was made up primarily of Slavic nationality groups. The Russians made up the largest group, and the Ukrainians, who lived in the southern part of Russia, were the second largest. The Byelorussians were the third largest Slavic group.

Many other peoples lived in Russia during this time, including Uzbeks, Tartars, Finno-Ugric peoples, Germans, Jews, Armenians, and Georgians. The official language of Russia was Russian. The language is written in the Russian Cyrillic alphabet, which has 33 letters.

During the 1800's, the arts flourished. Outstanding writers and composers created some of the world's greatest literary and musical classics.

10

Branches frame a serene view of the snow-covered Ipatyevsky Monastery, a cloister near the city of Kostroma.

This was the era of writers such as Alexander Pushkin, Fyodor Dostoevsky, Anton Chekhov, and Leo Tolstoy. Russian composers of the period included Mikhail Glinka, the father of serious Russian music; Modest Mussorgsky; Nikolai Rimsky-Korsakov; Sergei Rachmaninoff; and Peter Tchaikovsky. Rimsky-Korsakov wrote an opera called *Snegurochka* (The Snow Maiden) based on a play by Alexander Ostrovsky.

The Snow Maiden would later become a popular figure in Russian winter celebrations.

By the turn of the century, living conditions for much of the population were very poor. A series of bad harvests had caused starvation among the peasants. In addition, as industrialization increased, there was growing discontent among the rising middle class and workers in the cities. Conditions deteriorated to the degree that, in 1905, thousands of unarmed workers marched to the czar's palace to ask for reform. Government troops fired on the crowd, and hundreds were killed or injured. After this, the revolutionary movement gained strength and eventually led to the overthrow of czarist rule in 1917.

This icon, depicting the Nativity of Christ, is thought to have been created in the early 15th century by Andrei Rublev. It is now displayed in the Cathedral of the Annunciation in Moscow's Kremlin. Icons like this one decorated many Russian Orthodox churches in old Russia.

Christmas in old Russia was a mixture of European customs and ancient Russian traditions, of Christianity and superstition, and of holy nights and strange spirits.

Sviatki in old Russia was a time for magical rituals rather than merry celebrations. During Sviatki, Russian people performed rituals that were believed to bring good health and good fortune to the entire family during the upcoming year. Evil spirits had to be guarded against, harvests had to be protected, and specific rituals had to be followed if one hoped to be safe in the world. Some rituals were thought to predict the future, while others were believed to prevent misfortune. To many, Sviatki was both a holy and a frightening time. The nights were especially fearsome, as spirits were thought to roam around in the dark.

Many of the rituals were more light-hearted, however, particularly those dealing with whether, when, and whom a girl would marry. Girls of marriageable age delighted in these divination games. Young ladies from noble families enjoyed the guessing games as much as servants and peasant girls did. A girl could use several methods to learn the identity of her future spouse. For example, she could pour hot wax into water and see what shapes it formed. The shapes would give her clues about the kind of man she would marry, or

Two young children put the finishing touches on a snowman in this Christmas card from old Russia.

13

name is. (According to folklore, this would be the name of her future husband.) But the stranger replies with an old-fashioned, oafish name. Dismayed, the young heroine gives up her divination for the night.

In rural areas, usually at midnight on Christmas Eve, girls of marriageable age threw one of their boots across the street. The first man to find a girl's boot would be her future husband. Needless to say, the girls kept a close watch to see which man, if any, picked up their boot.

Young women in other parts of Russia lit a candle in front of a mirror, again at the stroke of midnight on Christmas Eve. If they were lucky, the face of their future spouse would appear in the mirror. And people sometimes hired an old woman who was good at fortunetelling. According to folklore, she used a black chicken to foretell the future. She

foretell the time of year she would meet him. Or a girl could run outdoors at night, holding a mirror up high to see if her future husband's face appeared in the glass. In *War and Peace,* one of the heroines does exactly that. She runs outside in the cold air dressed in her evening gown, but all she sees in her mirror is the moon. Disappointed, she tries another method, and asks the first man she meets on the street what his simply let the chicken loose in the yard, and, supposedly, it would run in the direction of the girl's future fiancé. If the chicken didn't go anywhere, it meant the girl would not marry. The chicken could also predict what kind of life the girl would have. For instance, if it ran toward a wheat field, the girl would marry a good provider. But if it ran toward a plow, it meant the girl would have to work hard for her living.

Many people sang *podbliudnye* (prophetic songs) during the Yule-

The singing of the kolyadki *(Russian Christmas carols) during the Christmas season is one of the oldest of all Russian traditions. The custom, which dates back to medieval times, was very popular in old Russia.*

tide season. In one such ritual, a bowl of water was set on a table and single girls were invited to place something personal—such as a ring, a pin, or an earring—in the bowl. The bowl was then covered with a cloth, and the girls sang prophetic songs while the objects were removed one at a time. The words being sung at the very moment a girl's ring or pin was removed were said to apply to that girl's future life.

Sviatki was a time of omens, signs, and predictions in old Russia. A frost predicted an excellent grain harvest, starry skies promised an abundant pea harvest, and cloudy skies meant cows would give plenty of milk. Other divination games determined who would live and who would die in the upcoming year.

Most of these quaint Russian traditions have died out, but a number of groups in Russia today are trying to bring them back before they are lost forever.

The singing of the *kolyadki* (Russian Christmas carols) during the Christmas season is one of the oldest of all Russian traditions. The custom, which dates back to medieval times, was very popular in old Russia. Young people bundled up and braved the cold, happily tromping through the streets of Moscow, singing the kolyadki. Kolyadki were originally folk songs that commemorated the renewal of the year. In later years, many of the kolyadki incorporated the Nativity and other Christmas themes.

Some kolyadki were magical songs—songs that had the power to bless or curse people. For example, when carolers sang the kolyadki to their neighbors, they carried bags that they expected to be filled with cookies and sweets. The carolers' songs said that if they were well treated, the host would have an abundance of cattle or crops. But if they were not given what they asked for, the harvest could be wormy and the crops might die. Sometimes the carolers asked for a pie, a cake, or some other treat, and if they weren't given one, they wished dire events upon the owner of the house. Usually they were rewarded for their efforts with sweets or other small gifts.

At Christmas, in old Russia, mummers like those described by Tolstoy roamed the streets at night, visiting their neighbors and amusing people with their antics. The mummers were often dressed up as animals—the goat, horse, and bear were particularly popular. Many mummers enjoyed dressing up as beggars and making so much noise that people claimed they could be heard as far away as Siberia. The mummers danced, made merry, performed various stunts, and generally tried to entertain everyone as they went from house to house. Historians believe the custom of mumming dates back to pre-Christian times, when pagan Slavs dressed up as spirits during festivities.

The Russian Orthodox Church frowned on many of the holiday folk customs—the mumming, the divination games, and the "fiendish" songs—but was unsuccessful in wiping them out. As Christianity gained dominance, the Christian customs were simply superimposed over the pagan rituals. The end result, as in many other countries, was a celebration that combined elements of both traditions.

The following is an example of a typical carol. The character Kolyada, *mentioned in the first line, is a personification of the* kolyadki.

Walks the Kolyada
on New Year's Eve,
and it searches
Boris' farm.
Boris' farm
is not big
and not small.
It's seventy milestones
by eighty versts.[1]
Sits the master,
shines the golden sun.
Sits the mistress,
glows and shines the moon.
Sit the children,
shine the many stars.
Who will give a dumpling
shall have many cattle.
Who will give a pie
shall have many calves.

[1] a Russian measure of length equal to 0.66288 miles or 1.067 kilometers.

Ornate, gilded woodworking adorns the 17th century altar of the Gleden Monastery of the Trinity. The monastery is in the city of Velikiy Ustyug, on the Sukhona River about 470 miles (760 kilometers) northeast of Moscow.

In old Russia, the Christmas season lasted a full 12 days to commemorate the time between Christ's birth and His baptism. The Russian Orthodox Church held special services every day during this holy season, and many devout Russians attended.

To many Russians, it was first and foremost a holy season. For 39 days before Christmas, many people abstained from certain foods. No meat was served during this period, and the day before Christmas, no food at all was eaten until the first star appeared in the sky. Young and old, peasant and aristocrat—and children especially—gazed into the night sky, hoping to be the first to spot the evening star. When it became apparent to all that the first star had indeed appeared, a 12-course dinner began—one course for each of the 12 days of Christmas. In some homes, straw or hay was spread on the dinner table on Christmas Eve. The straw or hay symbolized the manger in which Christ was born.

Fish was usually served—instead

of meat—at the Christmas Eve dinner, along with the traditional *kissel* (a mousselike berry dessert) and *borscht* (a rich soup made with cabbage, onions, potatoes, beets, and carrots), stuffed cabbage leaves, and *kutya,* the most important Christmas dish of all. Kutya is a rich, sweet porridge made of wheat berries, poppy seeds, and honey. The recipe is so old that no one knows its origins.

For centuries, Russians have served kutya on Christmas Eve. Many believed that kutya eaten from a single bowl on this holy night had the power to recall deceased ancestors. The single dish also symbolized unity to the peasants. Some families used to throw a spoonful of kutya up to the ceiling. According to tradition, if the kutya stuck, there would be a plentiful honey harvest. And if the kutya fell, it would no doubt stick to someone or something else. Everyone watched out if this was the case, for no one wanted this sticky substance on their hair or in their clothes.

The Christmas feasts of the nobles and landowners were often extravagant and sometimes opulent. Contemporary accounts tell of the lavish and fantastic dishes served at these affairs, and of one family who had enough gold plates to serve 1,000 guests. For centuries, however, the food of the rich and poor varied more in quantity than in content. The rich spared no expense and served a feast that was truly fit for a czar. Their dec-

orations and gifts were equally lavish. Very young children were given elaborate stuffed toys. Girls were presented with ornately dressed dolls, and boys got toy soldiers and boats.

On Christmas Day, meat could be eaten at last, and mountains of food were prepared for all to enjoy—including duck, ham, goose, pig, and other roast meats. A suckling pig, stuffed with peas and buckwheat, was a favorite dish, as was pig's head. A bowl of borscht was almost always served, garnished with parsley or dill and a dash of sour cream. A platter of jellied sturgeon often graced the table. *Blini* was another popular dish; it consisted of feather-light buckwheat pancakes rolled with caviar and also served with sour cream. The holiday fare might also include such delicious dishes as *pelmeni,* miniature dumplings filled with beef and pork, and *piroshki* (savory, filled pastries).

Everybody ate as much as they possibly could. There was also plenty of tea and Russian vodka to drink. The Christmas dinner was traditionally a time for extended families to get together.

Religious services at Christmastime were also a must in Russia, and nearly everyone attended church. The beliefs of the Russian Orthodox Church are based upon the Bible and the *holy traditions,* a set of doctrines dating from the early days of Christianity. *Icons,* religious paintings that are considered sacred, adorn

The Madonna of Vladimir is one of Russia's most revered icons. It first went on display in Moscow's Kremlin in 1395, and it is said to have shielded the city from attack on three separate occasions.

many Orthodox churches. They often depict *Bogoroditsa,* the mother of Christ. Worshipers often kissed the icons, knelt before them, and lit candles in front of them, especially during Christmas services. The Rus-sian Orthodox Church is also world renowned for its excellent religious music. At no time was this music more captivating than during holiday services.

The Russian word for going to

church is *otstoyat,* which means literally "to stand the service"—so called because there is standing room only in Russian Orthodox churches. In prerevolutionary Russia, there were no seats at all. Services were intended to mortify the flesh so that the soul could live on—they were not meant to be enjoyed. Today, benches line the walls of Russian Orthodox churches, but they are reserved for the very old, very young, very sick, and very pregnant.

In the old days, services started at 6 o'clock on Christmas Eve and often lasted for several hours. Christmas Day services began around noon, and again lasted for several hours. The churches were aglow with the light of thousands of tall pink candles. Sometimes members of the congregation held candles during services. Everyone joined in singing the ancient hymns, most received Communion, and people remembered the day the Savior was born.

Since medieval times, the Russian Orthodox Church has held Christmas services during Sviatki, and many Russian people revered the beautiful celebrations. These church services were a time-honored tradition and an integral part of Russian culture.

Although Christmas in Russia was never as commercialized as it became in the West, Christmas trees were popular throughout Russia in the 1800's. Three days before the big

event, fir trees went on sale in Moscow, and people searched for the finest one with as much enthusiasm as they do today. Most decorations were too expensive to buy, so people made their own. They hung apples and tan-

St. Nicholas of Myra is depicted in this 13th century Novgorod icon. Nicholas was a holy bishop of Myra in the 4th century, and is the patron saint of Russia.

gerines on the tree, along with little dolls made of dried fruit and candy. Walnuts were dipped in egg white, rolled in sheets of gold foil, and hung by silver threads. Often the whole family helped make these decorations, and children especially enjoyed making the little dolls. Many a father was enlisted to carve wooden ornaments—animals or dolls or characters from Russian folklore.

Sometimes small lanterns were made out of colored paper. These lanterns were too fragile to hold candles, but they added a festive touch. Some people made long chains out of brightly colored paper and strung them on the tree. And, of course, every Christmas tree was topped with a shining star, representing the star in the East that led the Three Wise Men to Bethlehem.

Decorations in the homes of the rich and aristocratic were much more

The Cathedral of Elijah the Prophet has stood on the central square of the city of Yaroslavl since it was built in 1647-1650. Yaroslavl, located 37 miles (60 kilometers) from Moscow, is nicknamed the "Florence of Russia" because of the many beautiful frescoes and ceramic ornaments in its churches.

elaborate. Etchings of the time show long tables with a dozen small Christmas trees on top and handsome gifts laid out for all to see.

The legend of *D'yed Moroz,* or Grandfather Frost, the Russian equivalent of Santa Claus, arose in the cities. It was said that Grandfather Frost lived deep in the woods of Russia and came to town in a sleigh. Unlike his Western counterpart, he did not come down the chimney (the houses in Russian cities had no fireplaces). However, he did make house calls — delivering toys and gifts door-to-door. Grandfather Frost had a reputation for bringing gifts to good children and forgetting those who were naughty. He could be both jolly and cold-hearted. During the Christmas season, he would roam the streets, handing out toys to well-behaved children — and overlooking those who had behaved badly.

Traditionally, Grandfather Frost wore a red coat and hat trimmed in white fur. Sometimes his outfit made him look more like a wizard than the Santa Claus known in Europe. But, like Santa's, his beard was snow-white, bushy, and long.

Some children opened their gifts on Christmas Eve, but others were told that Grandfather Frost wouldn't come until they were fast asleep, and they would find their gifts under the tree on Christmas morning. Russian children of the 1800's looked forward to the arrival of Grandfather Frost every bit as much as Western children look forward to a visit from Santa Claus today.

In the countryside, the notion of Grandfather Frost was slower to

The popularity of Christmas trees is attested to in this old Russian Christmas post card, in which an angel carries her very own tree.

catch on. Most country people did not believe in such a gift-giver. But they had a tradition of the "Frost," or cold. They believed that if they invited the Frost into their homes and let him help himself to kissel and other treats, then he wouldn't "frost" their crops. No one had actually seen

ming, and Grandfather Frost, it was also a profoundly religious season. During Sviatki, people celebrated the birth of Jesus and their Christian

As this illustration from a holiday card shows, even Grandfather Frost relies on a troika in his travels through the cities and countryside of Russia.

this mythical character, and no one dressed up as the Frost, but it was a common folk tradition in the 1800's to lay out food for the Frost. Perhaps the legend of Grandfather Frost grew from this tradition, and over the years, he became more of a gift-giver.

Whether people lived in the city or the country, the Sviatki was a very important season. Although it was a time of parties, fortunetelling, mum-

heritage. In short, for most Russians, a year without Christmas would have been unthinkable. And yet, after nearly 1,000 years of Christianity, Christmas in Russia and all its ancient traditions would shortly be swept away.

Through the centuries, winter was a season when the Russian peasant celebrated. The year's work was finished, and rest and relaxation were the order of the day. It followed that Christmas and New Year's were the most popular holidays.

Before the time of czar Peter the Great, who ruled Russia in the late 1600's and early 1700's, Russians celebrated the start of the new year on September 1, according to the old Muscovy calendar. An old story tells how Peter and a large crowd of his *boyars* (high-ranking landowners) and officers celebrated New Year's early in his reign. Sitting at a long table, splitting apples, the men made one toast after another. Every time an officer lifted his glass in a toast, 25 guns were fired. The celebration continued long into the night.

But as early as 1699, in accordance with European tradition, Peter decreed that January 1 would be the official start of the new year in Russia. The czar faced some opposition, however. Many devout Russians claimed that God would never have created the world in the middle of winter. One anecdote says that Peter's response was to show them a globe of the world, pointing out that Russia was not the whole world, and that at the equator it was warm in winter. It was said that in those days, few were brave enough to argue with the czar, so Peter had his way.

To celebrate the change and firmly establish the new date in the minds of the Muscovites (as those who live in Moscow are often called), the czar ordered that special New Year's services be held at all the churches on January 1. He also borrowed many New Year's customs from the Europeans. He encouraged the Russian people to light bonfires on New Year's Eve, an idea that they readily adopted. He also instructed the people to decorate their doorposts and houses with festive evergreen branches. Then he commanded everyone to "display their happiness by loudly congratulating" their neigh-

> *In short, for most Russians, a year without Christmas would have been unthinkable. And yet, after nearly 1,000 years of Christianity, Christmas in Russia and all its ancient traditions would shortly be swept away.*

bors on the New Year. And he proclaimed that every Russian house was to be illuminated and open for feasting for seven full days. Thus began the tradition of an extended winter holiday season in Russia. Over the centuries, these customs became firmly entrenched in Russian culture, and there was much celebrating and well-wishing on New Year's Eve.

The Mummers' Holiday

The following scene, from Leo Tolstoy's War and Peace, *opens in the home of the Rostovs, an aristocratic family in 19th-century Russia. When the mummers arrive at the Rostov house, Natasha Rostov is singing, accompanied by her brother Nicholas on the clavichord. Their cousin Sonya is listening to the duo, as are Countess Rostov and Herr Dimmler. Suddenly, Natasha's younger brother Pétia bursts into the music room to announce to all that a party of mummers has arrived.*

All the servants had dressed up, some as bears, Turks, tavern-keepers, or fine ladies; all as comic or formidable characters. Bringing with them the chill of the night outside, they did not at first venture any farther than the hall, where they huddled together bashfully. By degrees, however, they took courage; pushing each other forward for self-protection, they all soon came into the music-room. Once there, their shyness thawed. They became expansively merry, and singing, dancing, and Christmas games were soon the order of the day. The countess, after looking at them and identifying them all, went back into the sitting-room, leaving her husband, whose beaming smile encouraged the mummers to enjoy themselves.

The young people had all vanished; but half an hour later an old noblewoman in a hoop skirt appeared on the scene: this was none other than Nicholas. Pétia was a Turkish girl; Dimmler was a clown;[1] Natasha was a hussar; and Sonya, a Circassian. Both Natasha and Sonya had blackened their eyebrows and given themselves mustaches with burnt cork.

After being received with well-feigned surprise and recognized more or less quickly, the young people, who were very proud of their costumes, unanimously declared that they must go show off their costumes elsewhere.

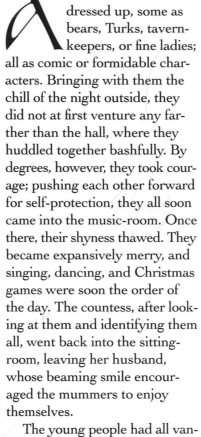

Nicholas, who was dying to go for a long drive in his troika, proposed that, as the roads were in splendid condition, they should go to his uncle's home.

"You will disturb the old man," said the countess. "Why, he doesn't even have room for you all to get into the house! If you must go out, you'd better go to the Mélyukovs'."

Madame Mélyukov was a widow living in the neighborhood. Her house, full of children of all ages, with tutors and governesses, was only four versts away from the Rostovs' house.

"A capital idea, my dear!" cried the count. "I will dress up in costume and go, too. I will wake them up, I warrant you!"

But this did not at all meet his wife's views: it was perfect madness! For him to go out with his gouty feet in such cold weather was sheer folly! The count gave in, and Madame Schoss volunteered to chaperone the girls. Sonya's was by far the most successful disguise; her fierce eyebrows and mustache were wonderfully becoming, her pretty features gained expression, and she wore the costume of a man with unexpected swagger and smartness. In her masculine attire, she seemed to be a different person.

Half an hour later, four sleighs with three horses abreast to each, their harness jingling with bells, drew up in a line before the porch steps, the runners creaking and crunching over the

[1] a light-armed cavalry soldier

frozen snow. Natasha was the first to tune her spirits to the pitch of the holiday gaiety. This mirth, in fact, proved highly infectious, and reached its height of tumult and excitement when the party went down the steps and packed themselves into the sleighs, laughing and shouting to each other at the top of their voices. Two of the sleighs were drawn by light cart horses. To the third the count's carriage horses were harnessed, and one of these was reputed to be a famous trotter from Orlov's stable. The fourth sleigh, with its rough-coated black shaft-horse, belonged to Nicholas. In his noblewoman's costume, over which he had thrown his hussar's cloak, fastened with a belt round the waist, he stood gathering up the reins. The moon was shining brightly, reflected in the metal of the harness and in the horses' anxious eyes as they turned their heads in amazement at the noisy group that clustered under the dark porch. Natasha, Sonya, and Madame Schoss, with two maids, got into Nicholas' sleigh; Dimmler and his wife, with Pétia, settled into the count's; and the rest of the mummers packed into the other two sleighs.

"Lead the way, Zakhar!" cried Nicholas to his father's coachman, promising himself the pleasure of outstripping him presently. The count's sleigh swayed and strained. Its runners, which the frost had already glued to the ground, creaked, the bells rang out, the horses pressed close to the shafts, and off they went over the glittering hard snow, flinging it up right and left like powdered sugar.

Nicholas started next and the others followed along the narrow way, with no less jingling and creaking. While they drove by the garden, the shadows of tall, bare trees lay on the road, blocking the bright moonlight. But as soon as they had left the garden behind them, the wide and spotless plain spread on all sides, its whiteness broken by myriads of flashing sparks and spangles of reflected light. Suddenly a rut caused the foremost sleigh to jolt violently, and then the others in succession. Then the troikas began to speed along the road, their intrusive clatter breaking the supreme and solemn silence of the night.

When they got out on the high road, beaten and plowed by horses' hoofs and polished with the tracks of sleighs, Nicholas' steeds began to tug at the reins and quicken their pace. The near horse, turning away his head, was galloping rather wildly, while the horse in the shafts swayed from side to side, pricking up his ears as if he questioned whether the moment for a dash had come. Zakhar's sleigh, lost in the distance, was

no more than a black spot on the white snow, and as it drew farther away, the ringing of the bells was fainter and fainter. Only the shouts and songs of the mummers rang through the calm, clear night.

"On you go, my beauties!" cried Nicholas, shaking the reins and raising his whip. The sleigh seemed to leap forward, but only the sharp air that cut their faces and the tugging of the two outer horses gave them any idea of the speed they were making. Nicholas glanced back at the other two drivers. They were shouting and urging their horses with cries and cracking of whips, so as not to be left behind. Nicholas' middle horse, swinging steadily along under the shaftbow, kept up his pace, quite ready to go twice as fast the moment he was called upon.

Nicholas' sleigh soon drew nearly even with the first one, and after going down a slope they came upon a wide crossroad running by the side of a meadow near a river.

"Where are we, I wonder," thought Nicholas. "This must be the Kosoy meadow. But no . . . I don't know where we are! It's not the Kosoy meadow or Dyomkin hill. It's someplace new and enchanted. Well, no matter!" And, shouting to his horses, he went straight ahead. Zakhar held back his horses for an instant and turned his face, all fringed with frost, to look at Nicholas, who came flying onward.

"Steady there, master!" cried the coachman, and leaning forward, with a click of his tongue he urged his horses to their utmost speed. A cloud of fine snow, kicked up by the horses, came showering down on the sleighs; the women squealed, and the two teams had a struggle for the lead, their shadows crossing and mingling on the snow. For a few minutes the sleighs raced side by side, but before long, in spite of all Zakhar could do, Nicholas gained on him and at last flew past him like a lightning flash.

Then Nicholas, moderating his speed, looked around. In front, behind, and on each side of him stretched the same magical scene, a plain strewn with stars and flooded with moonlight.

"To the left, Zakhar says . . . but why to the left?" thought Nicholas. "Aren't we going to the Mélyukovs'? Can this be the way to Mélyukovka? . . . But we are going where fate directs or as Heaven may guide us." Turning to the others, Nicholas asked, "It is all very strange and most delightful, isn't it?"

"Oh! Look at his eyelashes and beard, they are quite white!"

exclaimed one of the sweet young "men" with penciled mustaches and arched eyebrows.

"I believe that is Natasha," thought Nicholas. "And that little Circassian—who is she? I don't know her, but I love her." "Aren't you frozen?" he called out to his companions. Their answer was a shout of laughter.

"This gets better and better," said Nicholas to himself. "Now we are in an enchanted forest—the black shadows lie across a flooring of diamonds and mix with the sparkling of gems. That might be a fairy palace, out there, built of large blocks of marble and jeweled tiles. Did I not hear the howl of wild beasts in the distance? . . .Could it be Mélyukovka that I am coming to after all? On my word, it would be no less than miraculous to have reached port after steering so completely at random!"

It was, in fact, Mélyukovka, for he could see the house servants coming out on the balcony with lights, and then down to meet them, only too glad of this unexpected diversion.

"Who's there?" a voice asked from the front door.

"The mummers from Count Rostov's—I recognize his horses," replied several servants.

Pelageya Danilovna Mélyukov, a stout and commanding woman in spectacles and a flowing dressing-gown, was sitting in her drawing-room surrounded by her children, whom she was doing her best to amuse, when steps and voices were heard in the anteroom. Hussars, witches, clowns, and bears were rubbing their faces, which were numbed by the cold, or shaking the snow off their clothes. As soon as they had cast off their furs, they rushed into the large drawing-room. Dimmler the clown and Nicholas the noblewoman performed a dance, while the other mummers stood nearby and the children shouted and jumped about them with glee.

"It is impossible to know who is who—can that really be Natasha? Look at her; doesn't she remind you of someone? Herr Dimmler, how fine you are and how beautifully you dance! And oh, that splendid Circassian—why, it is Sonya!—What a kind and delightful surprise; we were so desperately bored. Ha, ha! Look at that hussar over there! A real hussar, or a real monkey of a boy—which is he, I wonder? I cannot look at any of you without laughing. . . ." They all shouted and laughed and talked at once, at the top of their voices.

Natasha, to whom the young Mélyukovs were devoted, soon vanished with them to rooms at the back of the house. Burnt corks and various articles of men's clothing were brought to them and clutched by bare arms through a half-open door. Ten minutes later, all the young people of the house rejoined the company, equally unrecognizable.

Madame Mélyukov, coming and going among them all with her spectacles on her nose and a quiet smile, had seats arranged and refreshments laid out for the visitors, masters and servants alike. With a suppressed smile, she looked straight in the face of each in turn, recognizing no one of the motley crew—not the Rostovs, nor Dimmler, nor even her own children, nor her late husband's clothes that the children wore.

"That one—who is she?" she asked the governess, stopping a Kazan Tartar who was, in fact, her own daughter. "One of the Rostovs, is it not? And you, gallant hussar—what regiment do you belong to?" she went on, addressing Natasha.

At the sight of some of the reckless dancing which the mummers performed under the shelter of their disguise, Madame Mélyukov could not help hiding her face in her handkerchief, while her huge body shook with uncontrollable laughter—the laugh of a kindly matron, frankly jovial and gay.

When they had danced all the national dances, ending with the *Horovody,* she placed everyone, both masters and servants, in a large circle, holding a cord with a ring and a ruble, and for a while they played games. An hour later, the costumes were the worse for wear and heat, and laughter had removed much of the charcoal. Then Madame Mélyukov could recognize the mummers, compliment them on the success of their disguises, and thank them for the amusement they had given her. Supper was served for the visitors in the drawing-room, and for the serfs in the ballroom.

Christmas in the Soviet Period

hen the first shot of the Russian revolution was fired in 1917, few realized that it heralded not only the death knell of the czars, but also the suppression of Christianity and Christmas in Russia. Throughout the 70-year rule of Communism, the religious celebration of Christmas was largely replaced by the Festival of Winter. Many traditions associated with Christmas were transferred to the New Year's holiday. The Christmas tree became a New Year's Eve tree. The Christmas dinner became a New Year's dinner. The Russian equivalent of Santa Claus—Grandfather Frost—arrived on New Year's Day. And New Year's Day

30

The painting February 17, 1917 *by Boris Kustodiev depicts the people's revolt in St. Petersburg.*

became a legal holiday, while Christmas was officially ignored.

When the Bolsheviks—members of the radical political party that became the Communist Party—switched to the Gregorian calendar in 1917, the Russian Orthodox Church continued to use the old Julian calendar, so Christmas in Russia was celebrated 13 days later—on January 7.

The change in calendars was not the only event that changed Christmas in Russia, however. The Communists who seized power in 1917 were *atheists* (they did not believe in God), and religious celebrations and rituals were not tolerated. Communists looked upon religion as an anti-Communist force and destroyed many churches or converted them into public buildings. Church leaders who refused to follow Communism were persecuted or arrested. Christmas could no longer be observed in the traditional manner—and it was dangerous to disobey. A Russian who attended church openly during this period could lose his job and jeopardize his chances for higher education. In spite of this, the Russian Orthodox Church had approximately 20 million to 40 million followers during the years of Communist rule.

Christmas celebrations were by no means the only aspect of Russian life to be altered. The revolution had a profound impact on nearly every facet of Russian life, including education, the arts, politics, and even family life.

The turmoil began with the "February Revolution" of 1917, when the people revolted against Nicholas II, then czar of Russia. Riots and strikes broke out in Petrograd over bread and coal shortages. Troops sent in to halt the uprising joined the people instead. In the weeks that followed, a new provisional government was

Throughout the 70-year rule of Communism, the religious celebration of Christmas was largely replaced by the Festival of Winter.

set up, and Nicholas II was forced to give up the throne. He and his family were imprisoned and reportedly shot in July 1918 by Bolshevik revolutionaries. Nicholas II was the last czar of Russia.

For a brief time, a socialist named Alexander F. Kerensky led Russia, but many people blamed him for failures in World War I (1914-1918), and eventually the Bolsheviks seized power and formed a new Russian government. Vladimir I. Ulyanov, more commonly known as Lenin, headed the Bolshevik Party—and therefore controlled the government of Russia. His party later became

Beautiful St. Isaac's Cathedral in St. Petersburg was spared from destruction by the Communists. The cathedral was built between 1818 and 1858 by Auguste Montferrant, and it is large enough to hold 14,000 people.

known as the Communist Party of the Soviet Union. They called themselves the Reds, for the color of the Communist flag.

From 1918 to 1920, civil war raged in Russia, with the anti-Communists, or Whites, fighting the Reds, or Communists. Eventually, the Communists won, but by then Russia had endured seven years of war, revolution, and civil war. Millions died from disease, war, or starvation. Finally, in December 1922, the Communist government established the *Soyuz Sovetskikh Sotsialisticheskikh Respublik* (Union of Soviet Socialist Republics or U.S.S.R.). The Soviet Union consisted of four republics: the Russian Republic, Byelorussia, Transcaucasia, and Ukraine. The Russian Republic—known as Russia today—was the largest and most powerful of the four.

The early Communists wanted to create a classless society, where no one had more than anyone else, and people were neither rich nor poor. To that end, they took over all privately owned industries, farms, shops, and other means of production. The Communists' ideology was summed up in their slogan, "From each according to his ability, to each according to his needs." From 1922 until the late 1980's, everything was controlled by the government, including the news media and broadcasting stations, schools, religion, and even the arts. Soviet citizens were not permitted to travel outside their country—or even move within it unless they obtained special permission. However, the government provided all its citizens with jobs, education, and free medical and hospital care.

Despite the years of repression, the Russian people accomplished a great deal. Between 1920 and 1980, Russia was transformed from a basically farming nation into an industrial giant, second only to the United States in the value of its manufactured products. Soviet scientists took the lead in space exploration with the launch of Sputnik 1 in 1957, shocking the world with the first spacecraft to circle the earth. The ballet dancers of the Bolshoi Theater in Moscow became world famous for their skill and gracefulness, and the Russians produced other formidable athletes as well. Most Soviets were proud of their country's accomplishments and deeply loved their native land.

During the years from 1920 through the late 1980's, the spirit of Christmas was not entirely eliminated. Although the official government position was atheistic, it occasionally relaxed its restrictions and allowed

some religious expression. Christmas services were still held in all remaining working churches, on January 6 and 7—Christmas Eve and Christmas Day in the Soviet Union. The congregation sang Christmas hymns that told of the Incarnation, and many churches were decorated with Christmas trees, icons, and colored lights. One newspaper reported that

In this illustration from the book Lenin and Children, *the former ruler is shown posing with a group of youngsters beside a "New Year's tree."*

The Nutcracker ballet, with music by Russian composer Peter Tchaikovsky, is a popular holiday production in Russia. This performance was put on by the Bolshoi Ballet, one of Russia's most highly regarded dance troupes.

these services "are regarded as a great evangelical opportunity." In addition to the public church services, many people observed the occasion privately in their homes. Friends were invited to share in a simple celebration and to wish each other *S Rozhdestvom Khristovym* (Merry Christmas). These were small gatherings, but they kept the meaning of Christmas alive on a grass-roots level throughout the years of the Communist regime.

After the private services ended, the celebrants might sit down to a huge Christmas dinner — a carry-over from prerevolutionary days when so many people abstained from meat before Christmas. The original meaning of some customs, such as eating kutya at the Christmas dinner, was forgotten. However, many others persisted in the hearts and minds of the people and would not be wiped out, no matter what the government decreed.

One such custom was decorating Christmas trees. In the first years after the revolution, the Bolsheviks banned Christmas trees. They declared that the traditional Christmas tree was a glaring symbol of reactionary rituals for which there was no place under the new regime. But the people were reluctant to part with their cherished winter holiday and its customs. The story goes that Joseph Stalin, then head of the Soviet Union, came up with a solution. In 1935, he lifted the ban on Christmas trees and decreed that they were now "New Year's trees."

Stalin then declared *Novyi God* (New Year's) a national family holiday. In effect, it was a sort of Christmas celebration without any Christian overtones. This compromise pleased the people, so a new tradition began in Russia. Many Russians put up New Year's trees on December 31, and left them up until January 13, or Old New Year's Eve, according to the old Julian calendar. In the Soviet Union, New Year's, for all practical

An extended family gathers around the table at Christmas dinner in the home of a Russian Orthodox priest in Yaroslavl. As in many other homes during the holiday season, a large, gaily decorated fir tree lends an air of festivity to the occasion.

Grandfather Frost helps a young couple select just the right tree at a fir tree bazaar in Moscow. During the Soviet period, Christmas trees were called "New Year's trees," and they remained a much-loved part of the holiday celebration.

purposes, became Christmas! It was a day for families to gather and share goodies, open presents under a brightly lit tree, and enjoy a big holiday feast.

Before long, New Year's evolved into the most popular of all official holidays in the Soviet Union, largely because it was free of dogma and propaganda—in sharp contrast to other government holidays. On May Day and Revolution Day, for example, the Communist message was apparent everywhere. But on New Year's, instead of sickles and hammers, there were brightly colored lights, fireworks, and champagne. Gifts were exchanged with much laughter and hugging, and there was always a lot of eating, drinking, and general merrymaking.

However, since Christmas now came after New Year's in the Soviet Union, much of its power was lost. People were often exhausted after New Year's, with little energy left for Christmas celebrations. And so many customs, like the trees that were once associated with Christmas, were now part of New Year's.

New Year's trees were inexpensive in the Soviet Union and were available to all. Some Russians preferred the artificial variety, which could be found in many shops during the holidays. Most, however, chose real fir trees, because of their natural pine scent. Fir trees grow in abundance all over Moscow and many other Russian cities and towns, and some of these firs are converted into New Year's trees.

Some of the largest New Year's trees were found in the town squares and plazas. These huge monoliths reached high into the air, their wide-spreading branches adorned with gigantic toys and dolls.

In Russian homes, toys and little dolls were also used to decorate the tree, as were colored lights and garlands. But the traditional star of the Magi was now the red star of the Soviets.

Another tradition carried over from prerevolutionary days was the legendary figure of Grandfather Frost, the Russian equivalent of Santa Claus. This gift-giver filled the same role in the Soviet period as he had previously, with a few changes. Now he arrived on New Year's Eve instead of December 25, and he was often dressed in a blue robe, not a red one.

During the Communist era, some parents hired students or actors from special service bureaus to dress up as Grandfather Frost and come to their homes on New Year's Eve, bringing gifts for the children. New Year's gifts might include books, small toys, or such practical items as clothes and shoes. Some children opened their gifts on New Year's Eve, while others waited until New Year's

Day and found that Grandfather Frost had left gifts under the New Year's tree.

During the Soviet years, another mythical figure, *Snegurochka* (the Snow Maiden) became a popular part of New Year's celebrations. As the granddaughter of Grandfather

A small child, bundled against the wintry weather, helps Grandfather Frost hold his staff in Moscow's Sokolniki Park.

Grandfather Frost, the Snow Maiden, and the New Year's Boy,
accompanied by a large and colorful cast, wave to the audience at a
1982 New Year's Day party in the Palace of Congresses.

Frost, she often accompanied him in parades and other New Year's events. Although she is often depicted with blonde braids and a long blue robe, the Snow Maiden sometimes wears a more modern costume — a short fur-trimmed coat, knee-high boots, and a white fur hat. Another figure in So-viet parades was the New Year's Boy, supposedly as young and fresh as the new year. It is almost as if the Rus-sians, having lost their holy family of Jesus, Mary, and Joseph, sought to create another family, consisting of Grandfather Frost, the Snow Maid-en, and the New Year's Boy.

Russia's Matrioshka dolls have become a virtual trademark for the nation. In the Soviet period, little cardboard decorations depicting Matrioshka dolls were often found on New Year's trees, and the dolls themselves were ever-popular as presents.

The Matrioshka dolls are a set of nesting or stacking dolls. Made from a thin, malleable wood, they are hollow on the inside and come apart at the waist. Each doll contains another, smaller doll inside it, except the last doll, which is very small indeed. A simple set may consist of six Matrioshka dolls, while the more elaborate and expensive ones may hold as many as a dozen dolls. These nesting dolls are popular throughout Russia, and though they seem to have been around forever, they are actually a rather recent arrival, dating back no more than 100 years. The dolls were probably inspired by the Japanese, whose beautiful painted nesting boxes were much sought after in the West during the late 1800's.

The classic Matrioshka doll is designed to resemble a robust, healthy-looking woman. The dolls wear the type of headscarf popular among Russian women. Typically, a Matrioshka doll is plump and curvaceous, with a cheerful, rosy-cheeked face. A shawl is painted on her shoulders, and her voluminous peasant skirt covers a rather round body. The dolls inside may have younger faces and costumes, representing several generations. Some sets feature "grandfather" dolls, but the "little mother" sets hold first place in Russian hearts.

39

Matrioshka dolls, which are internationally recognized, are a popular gift year-round in Russia.

Other New Year's Day gifts might have included books, small toys, or such practical items as clothes and shoes. Electronic toys were hard to come by in the Soviet Union and were not frequently given as Christmas presents.

After the presents were opened, many families sat down to a New Year's Eve feast. In the Soviet period, Russians managed to procure the ingredients for a substantial meal in spite of widespread food shortages. Perseverance, friends, or other connections might have helped yield the sought-after components, and people also gathered supplies well in advance for special occasions.

The all-night feast might have included such delectable treats as caviar, or smoked fish and roast meats if the family could afford them. There might have been a roast stuffed suckling pig at center stage—a traditional main course for many families.

Karavay was another favorite holiday food. This round bread was usually made from wheat or rye flour. It was baked in a huge oven, and the final product was so big it sometimes

Shoppers wait in line to buy Christmas candy in Moscow. Shortages of food and many other goods have made patience and perseverance necessary traits for consumers in Russia.

covered an entire table. (Today's karavay is about the size of a loaf of Italian bread.)

Fresh fruits and vegetables have always been hard to find in Russia, especially in winter, but somehow they appeared on Russian tables on special occasions. Many cakes and sweets were also served during this season, including baba and a variety of cookies. *Baba,* a popular dessert in Russia, was often sold by street vendors. It is a raised coffeecake baked in a deep round pan. When rum is added, the dessert is called *rom-baba.* The name *baba,* which means "a robust woman," refers to the round, wide-skirted shape of the final cake.

A rich New Year's table was supposed to be an indication for the upcoming year. A lot of good food on New Year's Eve meant you would enjoy abundance all year long—and the reverse was also true. Therefore most Russians spared no expense to lay out a lavish spread on New Year's Eve.

Tradition demanded that Russians say good-by to the old year with a shot of vodka and welcome the new year with a glass of champagne. Russians claim that their vodka is the best in the world, and the world, in general, agrees with them.

Many toasts were heard over the clinking of glasses as friends and relatives wished each other *S Novym Godom* (Happy New Year). When the clock struck 12, the pop of a cork pierced the air, and everyone lifted glasses of champagne. (Former Soviet President Mikhail Gorbachev, hoping to reduce alcohol consumption in the Soviet Union, broke with this tradition during his presidency. He toasted the new year on a nationwide television broadcast with a glass of tea.) Many Russians stayed up all night on New Year's Eve, enjoying the company and good conversation of their friends.

The burden of preparing the holiday meal typically fell on women, and their duties were made even more difficult by the time they spent waiting in line at food stores. It was not unusual for a Russian woman to spend her lunch hours and precious after-work time waiting in line to buy just the basic necessities of life. During the holidays, the wait for special items and ingredients could be even longer, and there was no guarantee that the sought-after foodstuffs would be available.

Also, without the many gadgets and conveniences enjoyed in the West, an elaborate holiday feast required more work. However, the feast was all the more appreciated by the family, and was a source of great pride to the hostess. While the holiday meals served in the Soviet Union were hardly as extravagant as the lavish feasts of the rich in old Russia, the typical New Year's dinner included a variety of courses and an abundance of food.

41

New Year's Day was an official holiday during the Soviet period, and everyone had the day off. Schools closed for a two-week vacation in late December, and the Festival of Winter began. For two weeks, Russians pulled out all the stops, and there was a continual stream of activities throughout the vast country. The government sponsored numerous children's plays, parades, and other festivities. Many of these events were designed to welcome in the new year. Actors presented new theatrical productions and staged old favorites such as *Emperor Maximilian*, a play about a 19th-century ruler of Mexico. Many dance specials were broadcast on television. Friends and families got together at parties. Concert halls and clubs hosted operas and other special events. And mummers would make the rounds, entertaining friends and strangers alike, just as they did in old Russia.

In the Soviet period, folklore enthusiasts dressed in mummers' costumes during the Festival of Winter to keep the old tradition alive.

Of all the New Year's celebrations that took place in Russia during the Soviet period, none was more exciting than the children's party held within the unlikely walls of Moscow's Kremlin. The impressive Palace of Congresses, the center of government, was suddenly transformed into a fairyland. On New Year's Day, the huge hall was crowded with thousands of children. In the center, a New Year's tree towered 75 feet (22.8 meters). It

Behind two mummers, a group of folklorists dressed as soldiers performed a scene from the play Emperor Maximilian, *a farcical comedy popular in cities and villages alike.*

was beautifully decorated in the most extravagant European tradition with garlands, tinsel, glittering glass balls, and countless colored lights.

As many as 50,000 tickets were sold for this annual event—and this was something no child wanted to miss. The fun began the moment a child entered the hall. When they presented their tickets, children were given brightly wrapped surprises. Then they jockeyed for the best position to watch the arrival of Grandfather Frost. Parents often held smaller children on their shoulders to give them a better view of this eagerly awaited visitor. Grandfather Frost arrived at the Kremlin on a Sputnik-drawn sleigh or some other fantastic vehicle. His entrance was greeted with great fanfare, and he was accompanied by dozens of colorful attendants, including the Snow Maiden, snow bunnies, clowns, and hundreds of children—young boys dressed like serfs in traditional peasant tunics, baggy pants, and boots, and girls in old-time pinafores. It was a spectacular sight, guaranteed to bring a smile to every child's face.

At one end of the hall, folk dancers sprang into the limelight, and the entire troupe swayed and glided to the sound of the *balalaika* and *gusla,* stringed instruments popular in eastern Europe. Musicians and singers from faraway provinces presented their wonderful melodies, and the children of Moscow heard firsthand the incredible variety of music spawned in their homeland. The fun went on for hours, thanks to the combined talents of musicians, magicians, dancers, acrobats, tumblers, clowns, and the fantastic animal characters.

44

While the Kremlin party was primarily meant for younger Muscovites, older children were by no means forgotten. They had their own dances to go to, often held at schools, clubs, theaters, or union halls where delicious food was served and a wide variety of entertainment was featured. Everyone stayed up until the wee hours of the morning.

Throughout the vast stretches of the Soviet Union, people rang in the new year. Young and old gathered to celebrate at farm collectives, factories,

and mining communities, as well as villages, towns, and cities. New Year's trees were everywhere, along with festive lights, paper lanterns, and fragrant evergreen branches. Public buildings were decorated for the holiday, and the streets were dazzling with colored lights.

Old traditions die hard, and in the Soviet period many Russians still celebrated what they called "Old New Year's Eve." By this, they were referring to

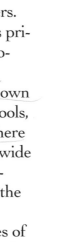

the date of New Year's Eve according to the old Julian calendar that was used in Russia before the 1917 revolution.

Many people found it difficult to make the transition from one calendar to another, and continued to celebrate New Year's on its "old" date— what is now January 13. This was especially true for older Russians, who could remember the days when Old New Year's Eve was *the* New Year's Eve. Many others liked the idea of two celebrations, and they rang in the New Year twice—on January 1 and on January 13. The second celebration, however, was nowhere near as grand or festive as the first. It was a quieter occasion, with friends getting together to enjoy a quiet dinner or go out to the movies.

Once Old New Year's Eve had passed, the holiday season was definitely over. Families took down their New Year's trees, children went back to school, and adults went back to work.

A highlight of the holiday festivities during the Soviet period was the New Year's Day celebration at Moscow's Palace of Congresses. There, Grandfather Frost and the Snow Maiden, accompanied by musicians, dancers, and figures from folklore, entertained an elated audience of children and adults.

The Legend of the Snow Maiden

Numerous versions of the story of Snegurochka *(The Snow Maiden) are told in Russia. The following tale was related by the famous Russian storyteller Alexander Afanasiev.*

A very long time ago, in the forests of Russia, there lived a peasant named Ivan and his wife, Maria. Although they had many friends and loved each other very much, they were unhappy because they had no children. More than anything else in the world, they wanted a son or daughter they could laugh and play with. One winter day, they stood watching children play in the forest. The children were having a great time romping in the snow, building a snowman, and throwing snowballs. Suddenly Ivan turned to his wife and said, "The children are having such fun making a snowman, let's build one too." So these two good people went out into the forest and started making a person out of snow.

Maria then said to Ivan, "Husband, since we have no children of our own, let us make a snow girl." Ivan agreed, and they proceeded to craft a pretty little maiden out of snow. They rolled the snow into dainty little hands and feet, then gave the snow maiden braids and little eyes and a petite nose and mouth. When they were done, they thought they had never seen such a pretty little girl. Struck with their own creation, Ivan said, "Little snow maiden, speak to me," and Maria exclaimed, "Yes, come to life so you can play and romp like the other children!" Before long, they noticed that the snow maiden's eyes began to flutter and her cheeks seemed to flush with a rosy color. At first they thought they must be imagining things, but soon a real little girl stood before them, with gleaming blue eyes and golden hair, in exactly the place where, only moments ago, a snow maiden had stood. At first they were too shocked to say anything and just stared at the little girl. Finally Ivan said, "Where do you come from? Who are you?"

"I have come from the land of winter, from the land of snow and ice and cold," the child replied. "I am your daughter, your own little girl." She ran to the couple and hugged them, and all three of them wept for joy. Soon the tears ended, and everyone was talking and laughing again, as this was the happiest moment of Ivan and Maria's life. At last they had a child of their own. They called to their neighbors in nearby huts and introduced them to their beautiful little girl, and everyone stayed up late that night, marveling over what had happened. There was much singing, dancing, and celebrating.

All the long Russian winter, the snow maiden played with the other children, and it seemed to the proud couple that their little girl was the prettiest of all.

Everyone loved the little snow maiden, as she was always sweet and happy and good. She would run and play and romp with the other children all day. Ivan and Maria were very happy.

But when the first signs of spring appeared, and the air grew warmer and the snow started to melt, the little girl seemed tired. She was no longer as lively; she even appeared to be unhappy.

One day she came to Ivan and Maria and sang a song, her eyes filled with tears:

*"The time has come for me to go
Away up North to the land of
snow."*

Her mother and father both begged her to stay, saying they would not let her leave, and they became so upset that they too began to cry. Ivan jumped up and shut the door to the hut so the snow maiden couldn't leave, and Maria hugged her tight. But as Maria held her little girl, the child started to melt away. Soon there was nothing left of the Snow Maiden except her white fur cap and white fur coat. Where the snow maiden had once stood, there was now only a puddle of water. Ivan and Maria wept bitterly.

Later they consoled themselves with the thought that maybe the snow maiden would return to them someday. But all summer long they were lonely, and could not bear to hear the laughter of other children. It reminded them of the little girl they believed they had lost forever. Summer turned into fall and fall into winter, and once again it was cold and icy outside. One night Ivan and Maria heard a knock on their door. The couple wondered who could be calling at that hour. Then they heard a familiar voice sing a song:

"Mother! Father! Open the door! The snow has brought me back once more!"

Ivan threw open the door and the snow maiden ran into the arms of her father and mother. All that winter she lived with them and played with the other village children. But in the spring, she had to go back North

to the land of cold and ice and snow, whence she had come. This time Ivan and Maria did not weep, knowing she would return once more when winter appeared on the land. And so it was that the snow maiden lived with the couple every winter, and left in spring.

Christmas in
the Russian
Renaissance

Winter traditions are enjoying a revival in the Russian Renaissance. Here, an appreciative audience watches as an artist sculpts an ice statue in a Moscow park.

n 1991, Russia saw a renaissance of freedom and openness—as if a door that was locked for more than 70 years suddenly had been opened. People finally were free to return to old, religious traditions and open their homes and lives to new holiday

the Russian people, celebrating Christmas was a novelty. Public celebrations of the holy holiday had long been forbidden.

Today, celebrating Christmas is no longer a novelty in Russia. It is fast becoming a part of people's lives. As the traditional ways of celebrating Christmas have been forgotten, Rus-

customs from all over the world. Free at last to express themselves, the Russian people welcomed back one of their most cherished celebrations—Christmas.

Russia enjoyed its first official Christmas in three-quarters of a century in 1991. To the vast majority of

sians are attempting to restore the old and creating new ways of marking the birth of the Christ Child.

Russians have always loved winter festivities. The revival of old traditions and the influx of goods and customs from other parts of the world have turned such festivities

24 — Ja 14

into a prolonged affair. Russians have incorporated the celebration of the Catholic Christmas into their winter holiday schedule. Winter festivities now begin on December 24 and last through January 14 — New Year's Day according to the old Julian calendar.

Many old Russian Christmas customs have been forgotten, and Western traditions have changed how Christmas is celebrated in Russia today. Western influences are apparent in the decoration of cities, the hanging of Christmas wreaths and lights, the singing of English Christmas carols, and the indulgence in nontraditional foods.

Revolutionary changes in Russian society began in the late 1980's, when Soviet leader Mikhail S. Gorbachev proposed a policy of *glasnost,* or openness, and initiated a program of economic reform known as *perestroika*. They have had far-reaching consequences.

In recent years social activity has flowered at all levels of society, with new unions, businesses, and banks cropping up daily. People now can

51

Present-day Russia is a vast region that covers 6,592,850 square miles (17,075,400 square kilometers). The country is bordered on the west and southwest by the other former Soviet republics. Within Russia lies the thinly populated region of Siberia.

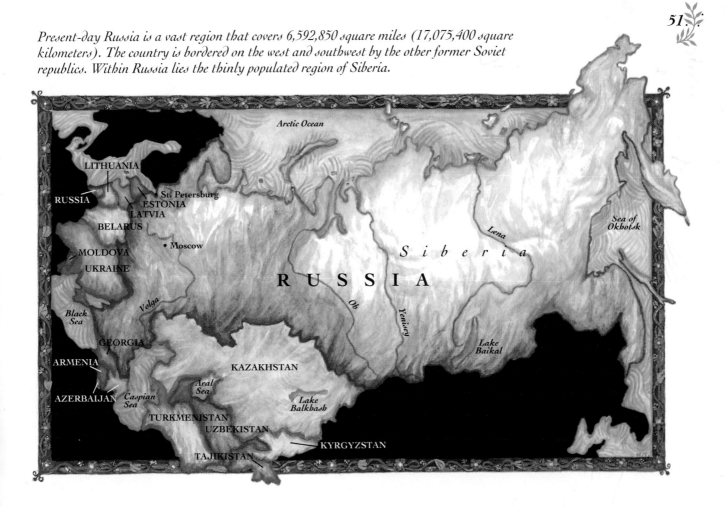

Shoppers choose among holiday decorations, toys, and handcrafted gift items at an open-air bazaar in the city of Kazan.

express their views freely. Writers and artists have creative freedom. Numerous areas of activity formerly controlled by the state are now run by private companies. People are free to travel to other countries and associate with foreigners. Religion is once again openly accepted—even encouraged—by the state.

The very boundaries of Russia have changed as a result of the Soviet Union's collapse. It was the largest country in the world in area and the sixth largest in population. With the demise of Communism, the 15 republics under Soviet control yearned for independence and have since broken away. Today the name Russia properly refers to the newly independent nation that was formerly one of the republics of the Soviet Union.

Once unleashed, glasnost and perestroika had a snowball effect. Radical changes soon took place in the political sphere of the Soviet Union, eventually forcing Gorbachev to resign. In June 1991, Boris Yeltsin became the first elected president of the Russian Republic. In September, the activities of the Communist Party were suspended. By December, the Russian Soviet Federative Socialist Republic became the independent nation of Russia, with Yeltsin as its leader.

The transition has been extremely difficult for the new Russian state. And while many questions remain about what kind of democracy Russia has today and whether it will work tomorrow, clearly a more free form of government has taken root in Russia.

The fall of the Communist regime has given freedom to Christians who want to celebrate Christmas and practice their faith openly. One of the most dramatic changes of the Russian Renaissance has been the government's position on religion. Not only has the new leadership of Russia given permission for the people to worship without reprisals, it is actively encouraging such behavior. The government hopes that religious ties will strengthen family life and restore old-fashioned values to society, thus holding the country together through a difficult period.

Millions of Russians have flocked back to the church. Some observers claim that half of Russia's 150 million people are practicing Christians today.

For many Russians, a return to religion represents a return to their old roots and their old culture. Visit an Orthodox or Catholic church, a synagogue, or a mosque in Russia today, and you will be impressed by the size of the congregation and the people whom you see. No longer are the majority of the worshipers older women. A growing number of men and young people are becoming regulars at church services. People feel

53

Worshipers fill this church in Moscow on January 6, Russian Christmas Eve. The Russian Renaissance has meant that the people can once again openly attend church services.

A poster of Grandfather Frost hangs from the entrance to Gorki Park in Moscow. Many public buildings now display Christmas decorations during the holiday season.

54 grateful that they can once again worship openly, without fear, but regret the gaps in their knowledge of religious traditions and lack of religious education.

Many churches continue to reopen throughout Russia, and thousands of new religious societies have registered with the government. Russia's new rich make financial contributions for reconstruction of old churches and the building of new ones. One of the most ambitious reconstruction projects has been the building of Christ the Savior Cathedral in Moscow, which was blown up on Joseph Stalin's orders in 1931. The building project started on Christmas Day of 1995, and consecration of the re-erected cathedral was held in the fall of 1997.

The Russian Orthodox Church, by far the largest religious institution in Russia, is the supreme authority in church teaching. Many of its rituals and services have remained unchanged for hundreds of years. It is headed by the patriarch of Moscow and All Russia, who is elected by the Local Council, a group that runs church affairs in conjunction with the Holy Synod.

Many other religious groups also worship within Russia. The Protestant population includes a sizable number of Baptists and Baptist churches. The Roman Catholic Church also has its share of followers, and there are many Muslims. In addition, Russia has more than a million Jews. Whatever the religious preferences of the people, they are now free to practice their faith.

Russia's winter festivals reflect the new face of the nation—the mixture of ethnically Russian traditions and the influences of other cultures, which the people now are at liberty to explore.

On New Year's Day, huge posters of Grandfather Frost hang in the Kremlin's halls and museums, giving the Kremlin a more festive atmosphere. Just as in previous years, there is a tall New Year's tree in Manezh Square in front of the Kremlin, gaily decorated with multi-colored lights and large peasant dolls. Lampposts are bedecked with blazing white lights and evergreen garlands, and electronic billboards flash New Year's greetings. Fireworks shoot boldly into the air from Red Square, illuminating its skyline of medieval towers and graceful onion domes. Thousands gather to drink champagne, sing, and watch the colorful spectacle while they await the stroke of midnight from the chimes of the Spassky Tower. Many young Russians hold sparklers high over their heads. Here and there, groups of people dance in a circle with arms locked and legs kicked up. The sounds of a thousand hoots, whistles, cheers, and songs fill the air through the early hours of the morning.

New Year's remains the favorite holiday in Russia. In every part of the country, villages and towns spring to life and celebrate with fireworks, parties, and champagne. It is

55

Cheery decorations brighten the night sky at the entrance to a square near the Kazanka River in Kazan.

Grandfather Frost, the Snow Maiden, and their attendants welcome visitors to a New Year's festival in the countryside outside St. Petersburg.

56

a time for people to forget all their problems and hope for better fortune in the coming year.

However, new traditions are arising in Russia. A growing number of people can afford to spend the week before New Year's traveling to other parts of the world. Some are happy to pop their champagne corks on a Hawaiian beach or on a camel's back in Egypt. Others prefer to go skiing in Norway or take their children to Grandfather Frost's workshop in Finland. Hundreds of travel agencies offer affordable package deals that can whisk Russians away from their routine.

Jan 7
Jan 6
op

New Year's is certainly a happy time for Russian children, whether they stay at home or travel. They look forward to the abundance of candy, beautifully decorated Christmas trees, time spent with their families, and, of course, gifts. As in previous years, most children open their gifts on New Year's Eve. Others wait and open them on Christmas Eve (January 6 in Russia).

Some lucky children are among the thousands who participate in the spectacular New Year's Day party at the Kremlin. Here they can watch Grandfather Frost arrive in a fantasy vehicle that resembles Sputnik or some imaginary contraption. Then comes the Snow Maiden, with her beautiful blonde braids and blue gown, leading a procession of young girls dressed as snowflakes in dazzling white robes and glittering headdresses. After that, a parade of singers, clowns, dancers, and musicians perform for the children.

With the development of advertising and marketing in Russia, children no longer have to wait for New Year's Eve or New Year's Day to see Grandfather Frost, as in times past. Today Grandfather Frost and the Snow Maiden can be seen a lot more often throughout the holiday season. They appear in television commercials and on billboards. And the two can be spotted in stores and supermarkets. Naturally this heightened commercialism has had some effect on the youngsters' view of these holiday characters. While they were once less skeptical if they encountered multiple Grandfather Frosts during the holiday season, there are many more skeptics among them today. Though many still overlook these coincidences in their desire to believe in the magic of the season,

At Moscow's GUM department store, throngs of shoppers admire the towering holiday tree and festive decorations.

the hardships that Russia has faced over the recent years have not left the children unaffected.

The winter holiday is fast becoming a way for creative Russians to make money. In the past, most families just bought a tree on the side of the road. If they got there early enough, they could take home a plump and fragrant one. Today, those who can afford it hire a consultant who will provide them with the exact type of tree they desire—from its height and color to the direction of its branches. Christmas wreaths, new to the Russian celebration of Christmas, can now be purchased at specialty stores or flower shops. They are quickly becoming a popular holiday decoration.

New Year's is, of course, an excellent excuse to host a feast, and many Russians do so with great enthusiasm. Many of the dishes of old Russia still make an appearance. These include borscht, blini, sturgeon, halibut, or

A Russian family enjoys a sumptuous dessert on New Year's Eve. The holiday meal can last for hours, ending well after the New Year has been welcomed in.

Patriarch Alexi II leads a special Christmas service in the Cathedral of the Assumption. The Cathedral is situated on the Kremlin's Cathedral Square, which is also the site of the Cathedral of the Annunciation, Cathedral of the Twelve Apostles, and Cathedral of the Archangel.

herring. Sweets might include baba, a lavish cake, or kissel. Children enjoy fresh fruit, wonderful cakes decorated with winter themes, and candy. Loaves of delicious Russian bread almost certainly grace the festive table. Russians still eat bread with almost every meal.

Ever since 1699, when Peter the Great made January 1 the first day of the new year, the Russian people have enjoyed this loud, exuberant holiday. In Russia today, New Year's is still a more important celebration than Christmas—the influence of 70 years of Communism cannot be wiped out overnight. But without question, Christmas is making a strong comeback.

Throughout Russia, churches hold Christmas services. Those of the Russian Orthodox Church are renowned for their sacred music. The works of many famous Russian composers illuminate the services, including compositions by Dmitrii Bortnianskii, Nikolai Rimsky-Korsakov, and Sergei Rachmaninoff. Some of these works, originally written for church services, are now gaining popularity and also can be heard in public concerts.

The glamorous old cathedrals make an ideal setting for Christmas services. They are always brightened with hundreds of tall, thin candles, hanging garlands, and icons that depict the Nativity.

Cameramen film Patriarch Alexi II, the Patriarch of Moscow and All Russia, leading a service on Christmas Eve. The service took place in Moscow's Cathedral of the Epiphany, also known as the Patriarchal Cathedral.

60

The priests themselves change from their traditional black attire to flowing, ankle-length, white robes embellished with gold embroidery. The patriarch of the Russian Orthodox Church and other members of the senior clergy wear special headdresses called miters at this time.

Christians who can't make it to church can now watch the service on Russian television. Many people prefer to stay at home because churches are so overcrowded during Midnight Mass on Christmas Eve. Even those who don't attend services during the year will go to church on this holy day. Every Christmas Eve (January 6 in Russia), the Orthodox church broadcasts special services from Moscow, other parts of Russia, and different corners of the globe where Orthodox congregations are also celebrating this holiday. The service is accompanied by a com-

mentary—a practice many people like, because they do not know the meanings of different parts of the elaborate service.

Recently, Patriarch Alexi II of Moscow and All Russia presided over a Christmas Eve service that was broadcast live from Christ the Savior Cathedral. The service also was attended by many important figures of local and federal government. Church services on high holidays today enjoy the same attendance as military parades did during the Soviet epoch. Government leaders attempt to fill the ideological gap in the country today with religion and patriotism. During the first Christmas service from Christ the Savior Cathedral, Alexi decried the growing gap between the rich and the poor and appealed to the Russian government to take care of the country's "weak and the unfortunate."

These days, Grandfather Frost works a double shift. He is around both on New Year's Day and on Russian Christmas. On Christmas Day 1997, for example, he was joined by his Western counterpart. Santa Claus flew in from Lapland for a historic "summit" meeting. The two bearded characters delighted hundreds of excited children gathered in the Kremlin Palace near Red Square. They signed a communiqué on strength-ening cooperation for the good of all the world's children and set up a "hotline" for future East-West relations. Santa, who extended his normal working schedule by two weeks to make this three-day visit, said that it would "put the final icing on the cake of East-West relations."

Thousands of churches throughout Russia are encircled by parishioners holding lit candles in a religious procession of Krestny Khod, which takes place after the Christ-

Santa, Grandfather Frost, and the Snow Maiden extend season's greetings to young and old at the Kremlin Palace.

61

On Red Square, members of the clergy lead the congregation on a candlelit procession known as the Krestny Khod. St. Basil's Cathedral, shining brightly against the night sky, stands behind them.

mas Eve service. The Krestny Khod is a Christian custom that dates back more than a thousand years and literally means "walking with the cross." Just as they did 100 years ago, the faithful proudly bear religious flags and icons. The highest-ranking member of the Russian Orthodox Church traditionally leads the Krestny Khod.

In spite of 70 years of religious oppression in Russia, the Krestny Khod was never forgotten. It was always observed on Christmas, wherever churches were open, as well as on certain other religious occasions, such as Easter.

The mood of the Krestny Khod is one of excitement mingled with reverence. The colorful and beautiful Christmas procession often takes place under the stars. Most Russians feel privileged to participate in this unique event. After the procession completes its circle around the local church, everyone goes back inside. The members of the congregation may sing some religious carols or hymns before going home for a late Christmas Eve dinner.

Many of the traditional Christmas foods of the past have long been forgotten and are no longer served. By the time Russian Christmas arrives, many people are tired after the New Year's festivities, so this holiday dinner is quieter. The Christmas table is normally less lavish than the New Year's feast. Everyday dishes, such as salted pickled mushrooms, herring, and various vegetable dishes, are served in abundance. There is usually an enticing display of homemade cookies. The only thing that distinguishes the Christmas dinner from any other meal is a candle set on the table. The Christmas dinner is usually eaten in the late afternoon after the family returns from church.

This kind of Christmas dinner may soon be a thing of the past, however. Russians are trying to restore Christmas traditions of yore. Christmas-dish competitions are becoming popular and are attended by the best chefs in Moscow, as well as lesser known chefs from Russia's 89 regions, some of whom still know the secrets of culinary Christmases past.

Though people usually exchange gifts on New Year's, not on Christmas, that also may be changing. Russians are trying to restore the traditions of their predecessors. The Museum of Folk and National Arts, for example, hosts an exhibit called "The Christmas Gift," which showcases the range of traditional Christmas gifts from different parts of Russia. They include brightly colored clay toys, forms for Russian gingerbreads and honey cakes, Chinese boxes with secret compartments, and other items that used to be popular Christmas offerings before the revolution.

In years past, the Christmas season was a time when the family sang kolyadki. However, no one knows these old songs anymore, except perhaps some who live in the most remote villages. The Bolsheviks made no attempts to suppress the kolyadki—they simply died out on their own. The songs are presented in some areas today by singers and actors in stage performances and are probably not typical of the impromptu singing of the past. No one knows whether the kolyadki will

This troika scene and portrait of the Madonna and child are two examples of holiday themes depicted in traditional Russian crafts—in this case, pysanky, or decorated eggs.

ever regain popularity in Russia. In the meantime, Christmas songs from Great Britain and America, such as "Jingle Bells," are heard in stores and played on Russian radio stations.

Christmas in Russia is an old holiday whose traditions have been

63

dissipated by decades of repression. Today's Christmas celebrations represent a mixture of the old, the new, the native, and the foreign. For example, though crèche scenes are not used in Orthodox churches, Russian artisans are beginning to make beautiful crèche scenes in purely Russian traditions of folk art. Christmas trees are decorated with traditional Russian candy and wooden toys, as well as Austrian crystal toys and pink, Victorian angels made of cardboard. The Christmas dinner consists of traditionally shaped Russian Christmas gingerbread and modern-day candy bars; cheeseburgers occupy the place of honor along with irreplaceable Russian pirozhki.

Russian parents, who grew up without religious celebrations, are especially interested in reviving the old and creating new traditions that their children will remember and pass along to generations to come. It is widely believed that if children don't acquire memories of joy and plenty, if they don't learn to put aside anger and meanness for even one day, if they don't learn the meanings behind religious observances early in life, they won't be kind or wise enough to face life's challenges honorably as adults.

A Moscow family enjoys a quiet Christmas dinner. After the hubbub of New Year's celebrations, the Christmas meal is a more intimate, subdued occasion.

Russian Crafts

Matrioshka Doll Hanging Ornament

This is a project inspired by the traditional Russian Matrioshka dolls (nesting dolls).

The ornament adopts the idea of "nesting" the different dolls within each other. This ornament adds a twist to the nesting doll idea by making these dolls a hanging ornament—each doll fits into another when the ornament is not hanging. Another twist is that you can personalize your ornament by making a doll for each member of your family, either by drawing the faces of your family members (and even your pet dog or cat) on each doll or by cutting out the faces of family members from photos and pasting them on each doll *(ask your adult partner about this first!)*.

Materials:

compass	crayons, colored pencils,
colored paper	markers, or poster paints
pencil	transparent tape
ruler	scissors
colored yarn	an adult partner
glitter	jingle bell (optional)
colored sequins	photos of family members
	(optional)

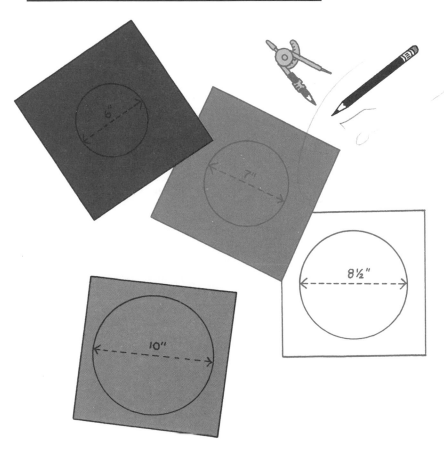

1. Using a compass, draw four circles on four different pieces of colored paper. The first circle should be 10" in diameter, the second one 8-1/2", the third one 7", and the fourth one 6". Next, using a ruler, draw a line to divide each circle in half. Carefully cut out each half-circle. Discard one half-circle of each color, or save them for another project. If you have more than four members in your family, you should start by drawing an amount of circles that matches the number of people in your family. The smallest circle should be no less than 6" in diameter. Cut out as many half-circles as you need, keeping in mind that each half-circle will be made into a cone that should fit into the next largest cone.

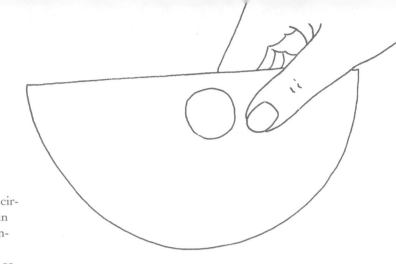

2. Take another piece of colored paper and draw four circles for the dolls' faces. The circles should be 1-1/2", 1-1/4", 1", and 3/4" in diameter for the four dolls previously mentioned. Carefully cut out the small circles and glue them onto the larger half-circles as shown. (Or, if you have been given permission to cut up a few photos, cut out faces of your family members and glue them onto the half-circles.)

3. Draw the faces of your family members on each of the small circles, using crayons, markers, or colored pencils. Don't forget to draw yourself!

4. You can add hair to each doll by drawing it on, or you can use yarn and glue as shown.

5. Give your dolls arms and hands by either drawing them on or cutting them out of colored paper and gluing them on.

6. Next, create clothes for your dolls. Decorate each doll, using crayons, markers, colored pencils, glitter, sequins, or whatever else you can think of—have fun! (Note: don't put any decorations on the straight-edge area of the cone that will be overlapped when making your cone—see illustration at right.)

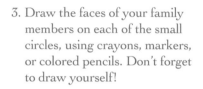

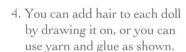

7. Now you need to make your doll "cones." Add glue to one half-circle as shown. Overlap the straight ends of the half-circle, press tightly together, and hold in this position until the paper stays together. (See illustration.) Repeat this step with the remaining half-circles.

8. Bend the tip of each cone over to the back of that cone. Secure the tip with a small piece of transparent tape or with a dab of glue under the bend.

9. Ask your adult partner to help you with this next step. Thread the large yarn needle with a piece of colored yarn, about 30" long. Tie a double knot on the long end of the yarn, 4 inches from the end. Working from the inside, take the smallest doll and pierce the bent-over tip of the cone with the threaded yarn needle. Draw the thread through the cone until you reach the knot. (Be careful not to make the hole in the cone too big.)

10. Tie another double knot in the yarn—4-1/4" from the top of the first doll. Pierce the tip of the next-smallest doll and draw the yarn through until you reach the double knot. Repeat this step until you have connected all the dolls.

11. When you have finished connecting the dolls, loop the top end of the yarn as shown and knot it close to the tip of the topmost and largest doll.

Now you have your very own hanging Matrioshka doll ornament! If you want, you can tie a jingle bell at the end of the yarn at the bottom of the smallest cone.

Grandfather Frost Tree-Topper

Grandfather Frost is a traditional figure in Russia. Now you can make your own Grandfather Frost decoration to put on the top of your Christmas tree.

Materials:

tracing paper
pencil
repositionable tape
colored paper
white glue
markers, colored pencils, or crayons
cotton balls
gold glitter
gold sticky stars or sequin stars
an empty toilet paper roll cut in half

1. Using tracing paper and a pencil, trace the Grandfather Frost pattern shown in green on this page. Also trace the patterns for the hands, as well as the oval that will be Grandfather Frost's face.

2. Tape the tracing paper to a piece of red or light blue colored paper and cut around the body pattern shape you traced. (Note: do not cut out the oval that will become the face.) Now you have the front of Grandfather Frost. To get the back, take the shape you just cut out and put it down on another piece of red or light blue paper, and trace around the pattern. Then cut out the back piece of Grandfather Frost.

3. Tape the patterns for the face and hands to a piece of pink paper. Carefully cut out the face and two hands.

4. Now you are ready to glue your pieces together. First, glue the pink paper oval face onto the front of Grandfather Frost. Next, glue the hands onto the inside of Grandfather Frost's back piece. (See illustration.) Last, put a thin line of glue around the edge of the inside of the back piece of Grandfather Frost, leaving the bottom edge unglued. Press the front piece down onto the back.

68

5. While the pieces are drying, you can continue decorating the outside of Grandfather Frost. First, draw his eyes, nose, and mouth on the pink oval with markers, colored pencils, or crayons. Next, put a dab of glue on the top of his head and spread it around where his furry hat would be. Take a few cotton balls, pull them apart, and press them down into the wet glue. Now put a dab of glue on the back of Grandfather Frost's head. Use a few more cotton balls, pulled apart, to finish the back of Grandfather Frost's hat.

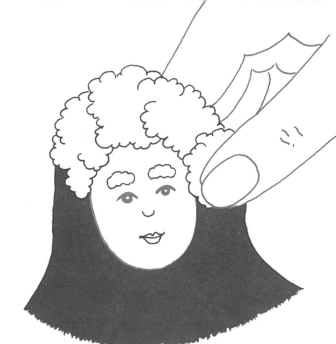

6. Add a little bit of glue to the area around Grandfather Frost's mouth and use more cotton balls to give him a beard and mustache. With a little bit more glue and more cotton balls, you can create furry cuffs on the sleeves and on the front closure and hem of Grandfather Frost's robe.

69

7. Finish decorating Grandfather Frost's robe using gold glitter and gold stars so that your figure looks like the one shown—or make up your own Grandfather Frost costume!

8. Take an empty toilet paper roll and have an adult help you to cut it in half. Put a little glue on the outside of the tube you cut and spread it all around with your finger. Open up the bottom of Grandfather Frost and stick the tube in until the end is even with the bottom of his robe. Press the front and back of the robe so that they stick to the tube. Hold the tube in position for a minute to set the glue.

Now you can put your very own Grandfather Frost at the top of your Christmas tree!

Russian Lacquer Box Gift Wrap

Painting lacquer boxes is a traditional Russian craft that is still practiced today. Each box is made of wood and painted by hand. Some of the boxes have very detailed designs and pictures that tell old folk stories, such as the story of the Snow Maiden. In this project, you will be able to make your Christmas presents look extra special by wrapping them up to look like lacquer boxes—you may even want to make one of these boxes to give as a gift!

Materials:
empty jewelry boxes (or other small- to medium-sized cardboard boxes)
scissors
black tissue paper or black wrapping paper
transparent tape
colored paper
markers, colored pencils, crayons, or poster paint
old magazines/catalogs
white glue
colored glitter
sequins
colored ribbon

1. Take an empty box and separately wrap the top and the bottom with the black paper. Be careful that the tape doesn't show too much on the outside of the box pieces.

PAPER SIZE

2. Now you are ready to decorate the lid of the box. Cut a piece of construction paper (any color except black) the same shape as the box top, but make the size a little bit smaller than the actual lid.

3. Next, draw or paint a picture on this piece of paper. Your picture can be a Christmas or winter scene, or a family portrait or picture of a favorite character from a book. Or, you can make a collage from pictures you find in magazines or catalogs (ask an adult for permission before you cut these up, though!). When you are finished making your picture, glue it to the top of your box.

4. To finish off your box, glue glitter, sequins, ribbons, or pieces of colored paper cut in interesting shapes onto the border of the picture you made. Do the same around the sides of the box top. Make sure all the glue dries before you put anything into the box.

And there you have it—the fanciest gift box ever, and you made it yourself!

# Russian Recipes

Kasha Stuffing for Roast Chicken

1 cup coarse kasha (buckwheat groats)
1 egg, slightly beaten
1 tsp. salt
1/8 tsp. freshly ground pepper
8 tbsp. butter
2 to 3 cups boiling water
2 cups onions, finely chopped
1/2 lb. fresh mushrooms, finely chopped

In a medium mixing bowl, toss the kasha and the egg together with a wooden spoon until the grains are well-coated. Transfer to a 12-inch frying pan and cook over moderate heat, stirring constantly, until kasha is lightly toasted and dry; do not allow to burn. Add the salt, 3 tbsp. of the butter, and 2 cups of boiling water. Stir thoroughly, cover the pan tightly, and reduce the heat to low. Simmer for about 20 minutes, stirring occasionally. If at the end of the 20 minutes the kasha seems dried out and is not yet tender, stir in the

72

additional cup of boiling water and cook covered 10 minutes more, or until water is absorbed and buckwheat grains are separate and fluffy. Remove the pan from the heat, remove the cover, and let set for 10 minutes.

While kasha is setting, melt 3 tbsp. of the butter in a 12-inch skillet over high heat. Lower the heat to medium and add the chopped onions. Cook for 2 to 3 minutes, stirring frequently, until the onions are soft and pale gold. Stir the onion into the kasha mixture. Melt the remaining 2 tbsp. of butter in the skillet over high heat. Add the mushrooms to the butter, reduce heat to medium, and cook 2 to 3 minutes, stirring frequently. Then raise the heat to high and cook mushrooms until all the liquid in the pan has evaporated. Stir the mushrooms into the kasha mixture and mix thoroughly. Stuffs one 4- to 5-lb. roasting chicken.

White Wine Sauce for Roast Chicken

2 tbsp. butter
1 tbsp. chopped onion or shallots
1 1/2 tbsp. flour
1/2 cup chicken stock
1/2 cup dry white wine
1/2 cup chopped chives
salt

Melt the butter in a saucepan over medium heat. Add the onions or shallots, and sauté until light yellow. Add the flour, stirring until smooth. Gradually add the chicken stock and wine, stirring until sauce is smooth and very hot. Add chives and salt to taste. Makes 1 cup of sauce.

Cabbage Soup (Shchi)

Serves 6 to 8

Stock:
1 lb. lean beef brisket
4 lb. beef marrow bones
1 large onion
1 large carrot
2 celery tops
6 sprigs of fresh parsley
6 sprigs of fresh dill
2 bay leaves

6 peppercorns
1 1/2 tsp. salt

Soup:
4 tbsp. butter
2 cups chopped onions
1 1/2 lb. shredded green cabbage
1 rib of celery, chopped
1 parsley root, scraped and cut
   into fine strips

1 lb. potatoes, peeled and diced
 into 1/4-inch pieces
4 medium tomatoes, peeled, seeded,
 and chopped
1 clove garlic, minced
salt and freshly ground black
 pepper to taste
fresh dill for garnish (optional)

Note: Cabbage soup is best when made a day in advance. You may store it, covered, in the refrigerator, and reheat it slowly when desired.

To make the stock: In a heavy 8-quart pot, bring the brisket, beef bones, and 4 quarts of water to a boil. Skim off any foam as it rises to the surface. Meanwhile, peel and quarter the onion, and peel the carrot. Tie the celery tops, parsley, dill, bay leaves, and peppercorns loosely in a piece of cheesecloth to make a bouquet garni. When the beef and water comes to a boil, add the bouquet garni and salt. Partially cover the pot, and reduce the heat to low. Simmer the mixture until the meat is tender, about 1 1/2 to 2 hours.

To make the soup: While the stock is simmering, prepare the vegetables as follows and set them aside. Shred the green cabbage, and chop the rib of celery. Scrape the parsley root and cut it into fine strips. Peel the potatoes and dice them into 1/4-inch pieces. Peel, seed, and chop the tomatoes. Then melt the butter in a 4-quart pot over moderate heat. Add the onions and cook until they are soft but not brown. Mix in the shredded cabbage, the celery, and the parsley root. Cover the pot, and simmer the mixture over low heat for 15 minutes. Set aside.

When stock is done, strain it through a fine sieve into a large clean bowl. Remove the meat and set aside. Discard the bones and bouquet garni. Using a large spoon, remove and discard as much of the surface fat as possible.

Cut the meat into bite-sized pieces. Add the stock, meat, and garlic to the pot containing the vegetable mixture. Partially cover, and simmer over moderate heat for 20 minutes. Then add potatoes and cook for 20 minutes more. Add the tomatoes and cook for 10 minutes. Add the salt and pepper to taste. Garnish with fresh dill if desired.

Siberian Meat Dumplings (Pelmeni)   Serves 6 to 8

Dough:
3 cups all-purpose flour, sifted
1 teaspoon salt
1 egg, slightly beaten
1 cup cold water

Filling:
2 tbsp. butter
3/4 lb. lean ground beef
1/4 lb. ground pork
1 large onion, minced
2 small cloves garlic, minced
1/4 cup cold water
1/2 tsp. salt
1/4 tsp. freshly ground black pepper

Additional ingredients:
1 egg white, lightly beaten
beef broth (optional)
melted butter (optional)
sour cream (optional)
fresh dill (optional)

In a large bowl, combine the flour and salt. Make a well in the center of the flour, and add the egg and water. Mix thoroughly until the mixture forms a ball. Place the dough on a floured surface and knead until smooth and no longer sticky (about 5 minutes). Cover loosely with a clean linen kitchen towel or wax paper, and set aside in a cool place for 30 minutes to 1 hour.

In a large frying pan, melt the butter. Add the onion and garlic, and sauté until lightly golden. In a large mixing bowl, combine the onions and garlic with the beef, pork, water, salt, and pepper; mix thoroughly. Cover loosely with plastic wrap and set aside.

Divide the reserved dough in half. On a floured surface, roll out half the dough to a thickness of about 1/16 inch; be careful not to tear the dough. Using a cookie cutter or the rim of a small glass, cut out as many 2-inch circles as you can.

Place a small amount of filling (slightly more than 1/2 tsp.) on the lower half of each dough circle. Lightly brush or spread a small amount of the beaten egg white around the edges of each dough circle, and fold over the top to join the edges. Press

the edges together with a fork to seal them. Set aside finished dumplings in a single layer on a plate or baking sheet. Repeat this process with the other half of the dough.

To cook the dumplings, bring 6 quarts of water to a boil in a large pot; add 1 tsp. salt. Drop in half the dumplings and gently boil, stirring occasionally, until the dumplings rise to the surface. This should take about 8 minutes; do not let the dumplings stick together while cooking. (When done, the filling will no longer be pink.)

Remove the dumplings with a slotted spoon and set in a colander to drain well. Repeat this process with the other half of the dumplings.

Dumplings may be served in heated beef broth, or drizzled with melted butter and topped with sour cream and fresh dill.

Kutya

Serves 6

1 cup wheat berries (whole)
4 cups milk, or more as needed
1/2 tsp. salt
1 cup honey
1 cup poppy seeds, ground in a coffee
    bean grinder or food processor
cinnamon

Place the wheat berries in a bowl and add enough water to cover them. Cover the bowl with plastic wrap and soak the wheat berries overnight. Drain them, then simmer them in 4 cups of milk with 1/2 tsp. salt until the wheat berries are tender (about 2 hours). While simmering, check the berries occasionally to make sure there is ample liquid in the pan; if necessary, add more milk.

When the wheat berries are tender, remove them from the heat and drain them. Place berries in a large bowl and set aside.

In a small saucepan, heat the honey over low heat and stir in the ground poppy seeds. Remove from heat.

Stir the honey and poppy seeds into the wheat berries, along with 1/2 to 3/4 cup of boiling water. The mixture should have a slightly soupy consistency. Place mixture in an ovenproof casserole and bake, uncovered, at 325 °F for 20 minutes.

Remove the casserole to a cooling rack, and let stand for 15 minutes. Sprinkle kutya lightly with cinnamon. Serve warm or chilled.

Variations: To this basic kutya recipe, you may add any or all of the following: 1/4 cup chopped dried apricots, 1/4 cup raisins, 1/4 cup toasted slivered almonds. These optional ingredients should be added to the wheat berry mixture just before baking.

Rom Baba

Cake:
1 envelope active dry yeast
6 tbsp. lukewarm water
   (105 °F to 115 °F)
1 tsp. salt
6 tbsp. sugar
6 tbsp. lukewarm milk
   (105 °F to 115 °F)
1/2 cup butter, melted and cooled
   to room temperature
5 eggs, lightly beaten
grated rind of one orange
3 cups all-purpose flour, sifted

Syrup:
1 1/4 cups water
2 1/2 cups sugar
1 1/3 cups rum

Sprinkle the yeast over the water in a large bowl, and stir until yeast is dissolved. Let stand about 5 minutes.

Add the salt, sugar, lukewarm milk, butter, eggs, and grated orange rind and beat with an electric mixer at medium-high speed until batter is smooth (about 4 minutes). Beat at medium speed for about 2 minutes more, adding flour gradually until all flour is thoroughly mixed in. Batter should be smooth and shiny.

Cover the bowl with a damp linen kitchen towel and let rise in a warm, draft-free place until batter has doubled in volume, about 1 hour.

Generously grease a 1 1/2-quart ring mold or bundt pan. Beat the risen dough for 2 minutes, then transfer it to the mold or bundt pan; it should fill the mold or pan halfway. Let the batter rise, uncovered, in a warm, draft-free place until it has doubled in volume, about 30 to 35 minutes. Batter should now reach the top of the mold or pan.

Preheat the oven to 425 °F. Bake the cake for 25 to 30 minutes, or until a cake tester comes out clean.

Run a knife around the edge of the mold or pan. Invert cake on a rack and let cool for at least 15 minutes.

While cake is cooling, prepare the syrup. In a small saucepan, combine the water and sugar. Simmer until the sugar is completely dissolved, about 10 minutes. Remove the pan from the heat; allow to cool slightly, then stir in the rum.

Place the cooled cake on a plate. Poke holes all over the cake with a skewer, then pour the syrup evenly all over the cake. Let stand; use a large spoon to baste the cake every 10 minutes with the syrup that collects on the plate. Repeat process until almost all the syrup is absorbed. Serve cake with whipped cream or vanilla ice cream.

75

Russian Carols

Let Us Praise Thee

English Lyric by Olga Paul

Arranged by Felix Guenther

Let us praise Thee, oh God in the heav-ens, Let us praise Thee. Let us

worship our Lord of the Earth, Let us wor - ship Him! May His

Praise God, Praise, Praise Him!

good ser - vants ne - ver grow old, Let us wor - ship Him. Let us

sing prais - es for our Lord, Let us sing prais - es for Him!

Kaleahdah Maleahdah

"Christmas Missmas"

N. Rimsky-Korsakov

Oh! Across the river there burns a fire,

On the bench a girl is sitting. Ka - le - ah - dah, ma - le - a - dah!

Kolyada, Kolyada

Father Christmas or Santa Claus

English Version by Cecil Cowdrey

Anonymous

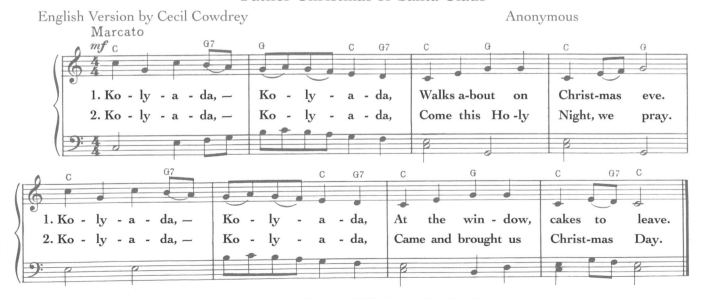

1. Ko - ly - a - da, — Ko - ly - a - da, Walks a-bout on Christ-mas eve.
2. Ko - ly - a - da, — Ko - ly - a - da, Come this Ho -ly Night, we pray.

1. Ko - ly - a - da, — Ko - ly - a - da, At the win - dow, cakes to leave.
2. Ko - ly - a - da, — Ko - ly - a - da, Came and brought us Christ-mas Day.

Glossary

baba (bä´ bə), a small, spongy, light cake, made with yeast.

balalaika (bal´ ə lī´ kə), a Russian musical instrument somewhat like a guitar, with a triangular body and usually with three strings.

blini (blin´ē), a very light, thin, small pancake, served with sour cream, or caviar, smoked salmon, or other delicacy.

Bogoroditsa (bəgər o´ ditsä), a Russian name for the mother of Christ.

borscht (bôrsht), a Russian soup consisting of meat stock, cabbage, beets, and potatoes, served with sour cream.

boyar (bo yar *or* boi´ ər), a member of a former high-ranking order of the Russian aristocracy.

D'yed Moroz (ded´ mə roz´), Grandfather Frost, a legendary Russian gift-giving figure who appears during the holiday season.

gadanie (gədä´ nēe), guessing games, often played in old Russia during the Christmas season in an attempt to foretell the future.

glasnost (gläs nôst´), a policy of open and public discussion of domestic issues encouraged by the former Soviet government.

gusla (güs´ lə), a Russian stringed musical instrument played by plucking.

karavay (kərəväi), a round bread made from rye or wheat, with designs on the top in the shape of animals, flowers, or other subjects.

kasha (kä´shə), coarse grains of buckwheat, barley, wheat, or millet.

kissel (kēsel´), a berry custard made with cranberries, strawberries, or raspberries.

kolyadki (kəlyäd´ kē), Russian carols sung during the Christmas season in old Russia.

krestny khod (krest´ nyi khôd), a religious procession that takes place on Christmas Eve.

kutya (kōōtyä´), a rich, sweet porridge made of wheat berries, poppy seeds, and honey.

matrioshka (mətryôsh´ kə), a particular kind of set of dolls, in which the dolls are graduated in size and "nest" inside each other.

Novyi God (nô´vyi god´), the Russian name for the New Year's holiday.

otstoyat (ətstəyät´), literally, "to stand the service"; the Russian phrase for attending a church service.

pelmeni (pēlme´ nē), miniature dumplings filled with beef and pork.

perestroika (perə stroi´kə), a major reform of Soviet society, especially in economic policy, during the 1980's.

piroshki (pirəshkēē), small turnovers stuffed with meat, fish, chicken, or egg and vegetables.

podbliudnye (pədblyōōd´ nye), Russian prophetic songs formerly sung during the Christmas season.

rom-baba (rôm´ bä´bə), a small, spongy, light cake, made with yeast and flavored with rum.

S Novym Godom (ss-nô´vem gô´dəm), the Russian words for "Happy New Year."

S Rozhdestvom Khristovym (ss-rəzhdestvôm khrēstô´vym), the Russian words for "Merry Christmas."

shchi (shchee´), a Russian cabbage soup, often made with meat, fish, grains, or vegetables.

Snegurochka (snigōō´rəchkə), the Snow Maiden; a legendary Russian figure sometimes said to be the granddaughter of Grandfather Frost.

Soyuz Sovetskikh Sotsialistich-eskikh Respublik (səyōōz´ sovets´kēkh sətsēəlē stē´chəskikh respōōb´lēk), the Russian phrase for "Union of Soviet Socialist Republics."

Sviatki (svyät´kē), the Christmas season in Russia; in old Russia, it lasted from December 25 to January 7. In present-day Russia, it lasts from January 7 to January 19.

troika (troi´kə), a Russian sleigh pulled by three horses harnessed abreast.

zakuski (zä küs´ kē), hors d'oeuvres; appetizers.

cknowledgments

Cover:© Uniphoto, artwork by Natalia G. Toreeva

1:	WORLD BOOK photo by Joann Seastrom
2:	Novosti from Gamma/Liaison
6-8:	Sovfoto
10-11:	The Great Encyclopedia of Russia Publishing House
12:	V. Solomatina
13:	The Great Encyclopedia of Russia Publishing House
16:	R. Koutcherov/The Great Encyclopedia of Russia Publishing House
18-22:	The Great Encyclopedia of Russia Publishing House
24-26:	Natalia G. Toreeva
28-30:	*27 February, 1917* by Boris Kustodiev/The Great Encyclopedia of Russia Publishing House
32:	The Great Encyclopedia of Russia Publishing House
33:	U. Rakootin
34-36:	The Great Encyclopedia of Russia Publishing House
37:	Novosti from Gamma/Liaison
38:	Tass from Sovfoto
39:	WORLD BOOK photo by Joann Seastrom
40:	© Andy Hernandez, Sipa Press
42-43:	The Great Encyclopedia of Russia Publishing House
44:	Tass from Sovfoto
47:	Natalia G. Toreeva
48-50:	Novosti from Sovfoto
51:	Natalia G. Toreeva
52:	© Rainer K. Lampinen
53:	Novosti from Sovfoto
54:	© Gary Henoch, Gamma/Liaison
55-56:	© Rainer K. Lampinen
57:	Liba Taylor, ANA
58:	© East News from Sipa Press
59:	The Great Encyclopedia of Russia Publishing House
60:	© Chip Hires, Gamma/Liaison
61:	Itar-Tass
62:	© East News from Sipa Press
63:	© Rainer K. Lampinen
64:	The Great Encyclopedia of Russia Publishing House
65-71:	Eileen Mueller Neill